Old Broughty Ferry
by Alan Brotchie

The ferry between Broughty and Newport was purchased by the Edinburgh and Northern Railway Company in 1845 and a new passenger vessel, the *Express*, was put on the service. However, to improve the facilities for goods traffic, an ingenious solution was created by the railway company's engineer, Thomas Bouch, who designed a double-ended vessel with rail tracks on its deck, on to which waggons could be run without difficulty. The most inspired part of the design was the moveable platform on the slipway which was raised or lowered to suit the state of the tide. The platform also carried two sets of rails, and ran on sixteen wheels on the slip, being moved into place by a steam winch. Two vessels were used on the passage, the *Leviathan* and the *Robert Napier*, giving a 24 hour service from 1851 until opening of the Tay railway bridge in 1878. Hurriedly brought back into use following the disastrous events of 28th December 1879, they remained in operation until 1887. It is thought that it is the *Robert Napier* which is seen here.

© Alan Brotchie, 2007
First published in the United Kingdom, 2007,
by Stenlake Publishing Ltd.
www.stenlake.co.uk
ISBN 9781840333947

Broughty's old windmill was a well-known local feature until the 1860s. Located just east of the castle (seen here on the left), in its latter years it was home and workshop to a carpenter. Its location is kept alive in today's Mill Street leading to the Esplanade. The windmill's location guaranteed an almost inexhaustible supply of wind – an energy source which is only now being acknowledged as one of nature's bounties – with no pollution and no nasty residues to pollute the planet. Today's wind farms with large numbers of monster industrial pylons seem light years away from this rural idyllic scene.

Broughty Station looking west from the footbridge in the 1860s. The Dundee and Arbroath Railway opened in 1838, initially as far as Craigie then to a terminus at Trades Lane in Dundee. At first it operated on a gauge of 5 feet 6 inches (as opposed to 'standard' gauge of 4ft 8½ins) but this was altered circa 1846. On the roofs of the old passenger carriages can be seen the 'pots' which contained oil lamps, the only form of illumination in the hours of darkness. Note the low level of the platforms and the generous distance between the tracks, a legacy of the early days of the wider gauge.

INTRODUCTION

Although a settlement has existed in the shadow of Broughty Castle for many centuries – the fifteenth century castle guarding (albeit sometimes not very successfully) the mouth of the River Tay and the wealth of Dundee lying less than two miles upstream – its separate existence as a Police Burgh lasted for forty-nine years only – from 1864 to 1913. This short life belies the feelings of strength of place which survive to this day. Broughty may have been enveloped by Dundee for ninety years and have theoretically lost its individuality, but today the sense of 'difference' is still tangible. The village of fisher folk in the lea of the castle grew only slowly until the early nineteenth century when, in 1801 and 1825, feuing plans were drawn up, the second being by David Neave for General Charles Hunter of Burnside. This latter plan introduced the regular grid pattern of parallel and perpendicular streets based around Queen and King Streets. Hunter himself became one of the first residents of the extended village, his residence, Red House at the east end of Beach Crescent, remaining a fine example of the handsome designs introduced then. The coming of the railway to this part of Scotland in 1838 immediately proved a boon for Dundonians who wanted to move away from beneath Dundee's frequent cover of smoke issuing from innumerable factory chimneys. Broughty became to Dundee what Portobello was to Edinburgh – an attractive coastal resort within easy reach of the adjoining city, and in the early 20th century the the village was estimated to have the greatest concentration of wealth in Scotland – more Rolls-Royce cars and millionaires to the square mile than anywhere else in the country. Electric trams, introduced in 1905, gave further impetus to population growth and speculative house construction, with Broughty's population growing rapidly from 3,513 in 1871 to just over 11,000 in 1913. That was a momentous year in the history of the Police Burgh, when, after a very hard fought action, Broughty's independence was lost and it became – for administration purposes – simply Wards 10 and 11 of Dundee Council, with just six out of a total of 34 Councillors. Broughty fought hard to preserve its freedom and ability to manage its own affairs, the matter eventually being taken as far as the House of Lords, but on 3rd November the deed was done and commemorated in ceremony and speeches. The ten-strong constabulary paraded for the last time, and was absorbed into the Dundee force. It may perhaps be no surprise that with the absorption Dundee became Scotland's third city, its population slightly exceeding that of Aberdeen. After abandonment of the local tramway system in 1931 housing construction continued and this development has ensured that the absorption is complete in a physical sense at least, with the former boundaries of today's Broughty impossible to distinguish.

This selection of photographs is largely from the collection of my late friend J J Herd. He had the benefit, in days past, of a close acquaintance with many people steeped in Broughty lore, and it may seem invidious to mention just one, the late Miss Agnes Pringle. Miss Pringle had her seamstress business in Brook Street for as many years as one could remember and was a fount of knowledge on all things regarding 'the Ferry'.

A sailing barque beached on the strand in front of Fisher Street in the mid-nineteenth century. The chute from the bulwarks is positioned to discharge the cargo into small one-horse carts alongside. Before railways took this trade, this was the manner by which most bulk cargoes were delivered – coal or lime from Charlestown, timber for builders or building materials like bricks were normally transported by coastal vessels such as this.

Commissioned and non-commissioned officers of the Tay squadron of the Royal Engineers Submarine Miners, with their Commanding Officer (Colonel Fergusson), photographed behind Broughty castle's gate. The service was started from 1871, but developed over several years and was responsible for underwater defence of Britain's ports by use of mines detonated electro-mechanically. A signal activated by a vessel striking a mine allowed the sapper watching to know which mine to blow up. The service also introduced the Brennan torpedo, the world's first guided torpedo. Only a third of the submarine miners were regular soldiers; the rest, including the Broughty contingent, were volunteers.

The Broughty Submarine Miners held an annual camp in tents on the Castle Green, with the sappers involved in rifle exercises. On the final day of camp large crowds gathered to watch the men parading complete with pipe bands. Open air dancing was organised and the day concluded with a firework display. In 1905 the service was transferred to be under the control of the Royal Navy, whereupon it was immediately disbanded. This was to prove a short-sighted economy as the port defence arrangements were reinstated at the end of 1914. The revival brought only limited benefit though, because in the intervening period the skills of the Submarine Miners had been lost.

The castle ramparts provided a convenient platform for local photographers, and many fascinating views of the village were made, from the earliest days of the camera. This record was made in 1883 and contains a wealth of fascinating sharp detail; to the right is the chimney of the local gas works. Dominant on the skyline is the bulk of Castleroy, built in 1867 and the status symbol home of the Gilroy family, owners of Tay Jute Works in Dundee. The equally pretentious Carbet Castle, domicile of the Grimond jute dynasty, can also be made out on the hillside. Both ultimately fell victim to dry-rot. The store building, centre foreground, may have been part of the shipbuilding yard which occupied this space prior to arrival of the railway. Likewise the barges in the foreground could be associated with work on the Tay Bridge. On the left can be seen the rail gantry for the Bouch designed train Ferry.

Looking west from the Castle and emphasising the strategic importance of its position. The centre of the scene records the heart of old Broughty, the smaller houses of the old fishing village contrasting with the larger, newer, Victorian constructions. Beach Terrace leads from the old pier to Broughty House, beside the railway pier built in 1848. A passenger train is standing at the pier station, hauled by a Caledonian Railway 0-4-2 locomotive. The railway here was built by the Dundee and Arbroath Railway, which from February 1880 lost its independence, thereafter jointly owned by the Caledonian Railway and the North British Railway. Operation was undertaken by the companies in alternate years. On the nearer (eastern) side of the pier can be seen the ramps used by the movable rail link gantries which linked the land-bound rails to those on board the waggon-carrying ferry boats to Newport in Fife. The 'Red House' is on the extreme right of the photograph.

Left: Another view by the same anonymous photographer, possibly taken on the same day. Behind is the *Jessie* and closer to the camera is DE 436, receiving the close attention of two extremely well-dressed, perhaps over-dressed, lads. Shoes were normally for Sunday wear only, but it is most unlikely that fisher folk would be at their boats on the Sabbath. The view gives a good idea of how difficult it would be to work these 'Fifie' type vessels without any protection from the weather.

Right: "Bathers" is the title given to this appealing nineteenth century view. The day must have been warm as there are several lads in the water. The fishing craft DE 435 is the *Thistle*, the operations on board being closely observed by an interested crowd of children.

Broughty abounded with the 'picturesque' and the area was popular with the early amateur and professional photographer. This image is from the same album of views as that of the old windmill, with several scenes included which date back to the 1860s. Broughty Ferry was home to line fishing, but with the growth of steam vessels line fishing became history. The Tay at Broughty Ferry was at that time also a centre for salmon fishing; in 1900 some 487 catches were recorded in the estuary. However, in that year the House of Lords banned 'toot and haul' fishing which brought Broughty's role in the industry abruptly to an end.

Unlike most photographs of this period, for once the photographer of this scene is not anonymous, as on the reverse it is noted that it was taken by W Bertie in 1894. Looking east from Beach Terrace, one of the earliest Victorian extensions of the old village, linking it up to the castle, the scene shows the assorted buildings which were added to accommodate the military garrison. Immediately to the left of the castle can be seen the rear of the old railway station, out of use since 1887.

A later panorama of Beach Terrace viewed from the old slip, with line fishing boats moored alongside. Volunteers regularly used the ordnance at the castle, using targets moored in the Tay with house owners told to open their windows to avoid breakage by the shock waves! After many years of complaints the War Office purchased Barry Links and target practice was moved there. The restrained architecture of Beach Crescent has now received a rude awakening with the imposition of an apartment block of unabashed modernity – in the face of many local objections, but with the blessing of the planners.

Castleroy again dominates the skyline, as it was designed to do, in this elevated view up St. Vincent Street. In front of Castleroy are the substantial Hermitage to the left and Camphill House on the right. The old school in the right foreground now serves as St. Aidan's Church Halls, while on the left can be seen the New Church of Scotland.

At the east end of Brook Street the roadway takes a 45 degree bend, for reasons which are not now immediately apparent. It was there that the street passed below the bridge carrying the harbour branch railway. Although the railway closed in 1887, the impediment to traffic remained for several years thereafter.

Broughty Ferry life, then as now, centred on Brook Street. In this view, looking east from the Westfield Road crossroads, the lad leaning in the doorway of Robertson's shop ('Branch of the Dundee Cycle Works' is emblazoned above the name) is keeping an eye on the photographer, no doubt with his large plate camera on a tripod occupying the centre of the street. The water cart has just passed, spraying the street on (presumably) a warm summer's day to lay the dust. The short stretch of shops on the left has since been swept away – there is certainly no shortage of small shops to be found to this day in the Ferry – replaced by a curiously designed modernistic block (which might have looked good on paper; or somewhere else!).

The rectangular grid pattern of Broughty Ferry is clearly demonstrated in many of these old views of the town centre. Despite more traffic the Brook Street buildings retain their individuality, and remain largely unaltered. One of the delights of the Ferry is the multitude of small shops, a feature which has not changed greatly in a hundred years. Note the policeman on the far side of the road, standing outside the branch of the North of Scotland Bank on Gray Street corner. With a force of ten crime was virtually unknown – prevention always better than cure.

This photograph by Alexander Wilson from about 1907 shows the corner of King Street and Gray Street. The pace of life was gentle enough and the novelty of a photographer's presence sufficient to draw the subjects' attention and stop them in their tracks long enough to be recorded for posterity.

From the crossroads, looking north up Gray Street from King Street towards the railway level crossing and the brae beyond Queen Street. The local lads have gathered to add some life to the photographer's composition – whether he wanted them or not. On the left a horse dray is making a delivery – of a non alcoholic variety – to the Lorne Bar (now the Ferry Inn) on the corner of Long Lane. Surprisingly it is from 'over the water' – from Melville of Tayport – rather than from Broughty's own aerated water manufacturer, Edwards of Camperdown Street.

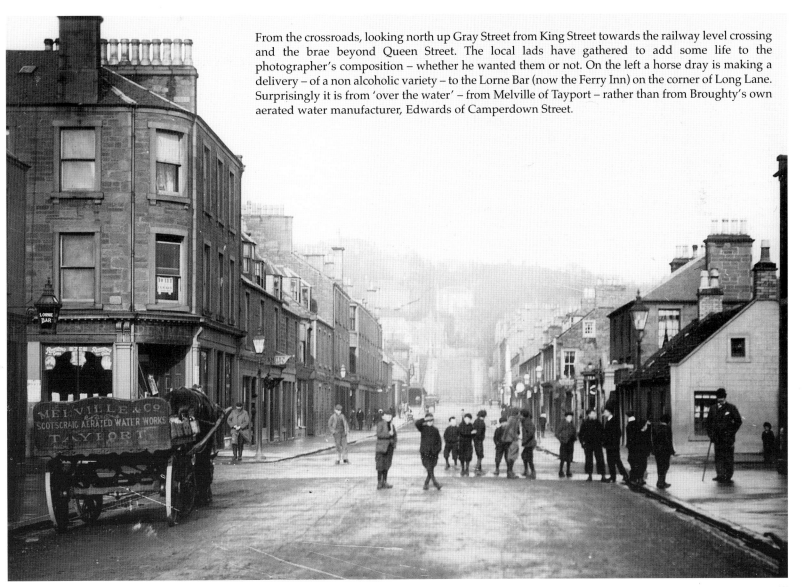

The Gladstone Place terraces at the east end of Brook Street are a good example of the housing constructed to accommodate the ever increasing population of the former fishing village. Development of housing was particularly noticeable following opening of the tramway line to Dundee in 1905. This event presaged a major growth in the numbers of 'commuters' to Dundee, those who wished to enjoy the benefits of living in Broughty, but of working in 'Juteopolis' and the tramway service was responsible for much of the expansion of the burgh which took place until the outbreak of the First World War.

On the left of this summer 1906 view of the junction of Gray and Queen Streets horse-drawn cabs are waiting to pick up fares arriving by train at the station, but holding centre stage is one of the (then) new tramcars, introduced from 27th December of the previous year. These trams, which ran from Dundee's Seagate, were operated not by the Corporation, but by the independent Dundee, Broughty Ferry and District Tramway Company.

The service from Dundee ran through Broughty Ferry to Monifieth, and was operated jointly by the Corporation and the Company. There was one Corporation tram to every three Company trams - a rough ratio of the length of the through route that each party owned. Both operators used cars of fundamentally similar design, the position of the destination indicator being the only distinguishing feature; this is a Corporation car. In this photograph, looking west along Queen Street, the two lads, probably heading back to the Eastern School, seem understandably anxious to get out of the way of the tram.

A train for Dundee approaches Broughty Ferry Station circa 1906, although most of the people on the platform seem more intrigued by the presence of the photographer than by the imminent arrival of the train. Stopping trains from Arbroath would terminate at the East Station in Dundee, but Aberdeen expresses would run through to Tay Bridge Station and then on through Fife to Edinburgh.

A passing glimpse of Broughty Ferry Station in the 1950s, from the window of an express from Aberdeen. A locomotive shunts on the goods sidings to the south of the line, the small yard used mostly by local coal merchants.

Prior to purchase of its motor units, the Broughty Fire Brigade had to rely on horse-drawn hose carts, with hired horses summoned by bell from Simpson's Victoria Stables in Gray Street. Its well-equipped fire station stood at the corner of Long Lane and Brown Street. The building, with its arches for the appliances clearly visible and with accommodation for firemen above, stood for many years until it was swept away. The site is the car park for the new Health Centre.

The carriage entrance to Castleroy, a view which only the privileged saw, although many local people have childhood memories of raiding the orchards for apples and pears. On the death of Mr. A B Gilroy in 1928 he allowed for his family to have life-rent of the building, but that thereafter, it and the grounds, were to be made over to the Local Authority and be used for a hospital or convalescent home. During World War 2 it was used by Polish forces then as emergency housing. It was found later to be riddled throughout with dry rot, and was demolished in 1956.

A dog-cart, on this occasion hauled by a goat, was owned by David Grimond of the Lorne Bar in Gray Street (now the Ferry Inn) - famous for its hot pies. Holding the head of the goat is a Mr Grant, a well-known music hall performer who was probably doing a summer season at Broughty beach and who lived in Broughty for some years after retirng.

In this beach scene from the summer of 1913, entertainment is being provided by the 'Bachelor Boys'. The best beach performers were said to be the 'Scarlet Merrions' – so popular with the "Nobs" from the big houses that they would take their seats at the beach in full evening dress – as if attending the theatre in Dundee!

This view on the left dates from Easter 1921. At weekends and during the holidays Broughty's beach was a magnet for the many who laboured in Dundee's mills. Every tram would be pressed into service and would run packed to capacity. All the local shops hoped for good weather to augment their takings as the Dundonians did not venture to Broughty Ferry when the weather was poor.

Annual events such as the sand castle competition whipped up great interest and attracted crowds to the beach. This attempt is of Dundee's Royal Arch – in the eyes of its creators – but we don't know if it won the prize.

Period piece photo on Broughty beach from 1928 or 1929 mis-captioned "lassies looking after donkeys", an insult to the ponies featured.

The beach was not the only attraction that Broughty had to offer. Orchar Park was obtained for the benefits of Broughty's inhabitants and visitors by former Provost of the Ferry, James Guthrie Orchar. He paid - from his own pocket - for the decorative railings with which the park was enclosed, perhaps to restrain lads such as these three (on the right) with their noses against the fence surrounding the bowling green. Orchar Park hit the headlines in February 1996 with the reported sighting there of a UFO – described as "burger shaped" and "like a rugby ball with lights"!

Broughty Esplanade looking south across the mouth of the River Tay to Tayport in Fife. Tayport was the southern end of the ferry which gave Broughty its name, a facility whose history is as old as the need to cross the Tay. Rugby Terrace on the right is still the final residential development of this area and this has allowed the links area and the beach front along this stretch to (so far) remain undeveloped and unspoiled.

Looking east along Dalhousie Road to Barnhill from the old railway bridge. This line took trains from Dundee to Forfar until the passenger rail link was closed from January 1955. The circuitous route to Forfar had never really justified its existence after the proliferation of motor bus services following the release of war surplus vehicles in 1919-20. This opportunity enabled many would-be transport entrepreneurs to start services without any infrastructure investment or such responsibility.

courtesy A.White

Development around Kerrington Crescent in Barnhill commenced at the very end of the 19th century, and continued in a quite leisurely fashion over the next two decades. Provision of the tramway in 1905 would be seen as a major benefit for commuting to Dundee, in the days long before every family aspired to own at least two automobiles. The photograph can be dated to soon after 1909, as it was in that year that this particular tramcar (Number 1 of the Company's fleet) received its covered top deck. Most Company trams remained unaltered until closure of the facility in May 1931.

Dalhousie Road from the railway bridge, immediately after cessation of the tram service in 1931. Track and overhead wiring are still in place in the photograph, but it was not long before the valuable copper overhead was removed. In the distance on the right is a Corporation bus, at the end of Balmossie Street, the eastern boundary of what had by then become Dundee. This was the limit of operation by the Corporation Transport Department.

Barnhill had other attractions, including a short golf course, definitely of the 'links' variety! Surprisingly Broughty did not rise to a course within its boundaries, Broughty Ferry Golf Club being founded, in April 1878 in Monifieth. The Barnhill club, for ladies only, opened in 1895. The short, but still 18 holes, course was unkindly known as the 'Tiddleylinks'! It was later reduced to nine holes, but fell into disuse during the Second World War. In its original state each player was allowed just one club, but after the reconstruction three were permitted – a driver, an iron and a putter! In the photograph, the small club house is on the left. The isolated building in the centre of the view is 'The Rowans', home of the Feathers family and the first building constructed in Collingwood Place.

The newly completed façade of the West End Garage at 28 Queen Street of Messrs Lawson and Stewart Ltd, in 1929. The growth of motor car use soon brought an end to the tram cars service. The tram rails and the stone setts surrounding them gave a rough ride to solid or pneumatic tyres. The setts extended eighteen inches outwith the tram rails. This area was maintained by the tram operators and its maintenance imposed a heavy cost burden on them, with the benefit being obtained by all road users. This legislative obligation dated back to the days of horse trams.

All makes were catered for by Lawson and Stewart in their new workshops – even down to the petrol lawn mower in the centre of the garage! The business is now a long established Honda franchise – a make unheard of in the 1920s. Soichiro Honda made racing cars before 1939, and founded his car construction company in 1947.

The monogram of the owner and proprietor of the New Grand Cinema in West King Street, V C Smith, was emblazoned above the front entrance, but in all likelihood patrons paid it scant attention, with their attention instead gripped by the 'main attraction'. The attendant page boy, as can be seen here, was properly and formally uniformed, complete with white gloves tucked below shoulder epaulets. The Grand Theatre dated from 1914, and was a handy retreat when not every day was sunny. It was reopened in this modernised style in 1931, closing just eight years later; housing now occupies the site. Broughty's first cinema was the 'Uno' in Lawrence Street, owned by Mr 'Eyebrows' Stewart (when most men were readily known by a nickname)

Despite the lack of traffic, the tram driver edging out of Claypotts Road at the 'Occidental Corner' is keeping a sharp lookout to his right. The scene might appear quiet, but at that time was a traffic black spot. At the beginning of December 1929, however, work had just commenced to ease the far corner in an endeavour to improve safety. The tram is of the same design as seen on page 31 of a style which was in vogue twenty years before, but by this date would have looked decidedly old-fashioned.

A late winter's day – March 21st 1930, looking eastwards at the same junction. The snow-covered tram lines can be seen over the hill to Brook Street. In such weather many passengers got comfort from the 'predictability' of the tram on its fixed rails unlike the not infrequent bus difficulties in frost or snow.

'Chicken Feed' may not have quite the same connotation as 'Poultry Food' but, however you want to describe the product, it amounted to the same thing! The Ferry had few industries, and certainly no heavy industries, thus enhancing the contrast with its larger neighbour to the west. R Easson & Company were obviously proud to have their new lorry photographed.

One of the several Broughty homes of the Gilroy dynasty and close to Castleroy was Dunalistair House in Hill Street, which became the Black Watch Memorial Home in memory of members of the local regiment who had given their lives in service of their country in the First World War. The regimental badge can be seen above and to the left of the front door. In 1984 the building was converted into self-contained flats.

The late Queen Mother was patron of the home and is seen here visiting during the year of her coronation, 1937. To her left is the Matron, Mrs Shepherd.

This photograph from around 1934 looks east across the Castle Green from that convenient viewpoint on the castle's battlements. All eyes are trained inland, to view decorated floats starting their journey through the town. In the foreground is a battery powered dust-cart, decorated florally by the Parks Department and soldiers who would be from the billets at the castle. The 'Windmill' bathing shelter perpetuates the memory of the long gone feature – but today still serves a 'convenient' function.

February 1936 and local fishermen took advantage of nature's bounty with enormous shoals of herring filling their nets.

ANNIE

Barnhill playground between the railway and the sand dunes. As far back as 1933 there were problems caused by the tide eroding the foundations of the swings, and it was thought that they should be moved to the landward side of the Esplanade. There are now more substantial childrens' amusements at the Castle Green.

No regular steamers to disturb the play potential of the Ferry Pier, the Slip, in the carefree summer days of 1948, a grand place still for a day's escape.

By the following summer two-piece bathing costumes had been spotted on the local beach to prove that Broughty had taken its place among the fashionable watering places of Europe. The two-piece 'Bikini' was then the leading edge of beach-wear fashion.

Above: On a bright day in February 1962 work has started on the rock gardens which were created on the site of the old Barnhill Ladies' Golf Course at the east end of the Esplanade. The gardener does not even lift his head to acknowledge the train passing on the main Aberdeen line behind him. An everyday sight then; the presence of a steam train here today would bring rail enthusiasts from far and near.

Below: Broughty Ferry's burgh boundaries encompassed another ancient Scottish castle – at Claypotts on the Arbroath Road. This nineteenth century photograph shows well the unusual Z-shaped keep built for James Strachan in the second half of the sixteenth century. The castle was sold to Sir William Graham of Claverhouse in 1620 (for 12,000 merks), but reverted to the Crown after the Battle of Killiecrankie in 1689. It was then granted to the Marquis of Douglas. In 1926 it was handed over to the Dept. of Works. One of the best preserved buildings of its date and style, these days it is open to the public. Like all castles it supposedly has a secret tunnel – tradition would have it that there was one linking Claypotts and Broughty Castles.

The north-west corner at Claypotts cross-roads was occupied by the Broughty Ferry and District Steam Laundry in the days before it became an accident black spot. This photograph was taken in October 1917 and shows a lady motor-cyclist, Dorothy Chalmers, negotiating the junction on her two-stroke Connaught machine. The Connaught marque was later revived as a racing car, which after World War 2 became the first British winner of the Grand Prix for over thirty years.

A later view at the same cross roads, opened out, but still a long way from today's traffic-light maze. Claypotts Castle can be seen on the far corner, the area from where this photograph was shot then a petrol filling station. Other than the castle, all the buildings seen have been swept away to allow various road improvements over the years.

The Woodlands Hotel croquet lawn has now given way to car parking, but the well-established business has fond memories for generations of Dundonians and Broughty residents as *the* place for family receptions.

On 3rd August 1934, the Royal Scots Greys made a brave sight as they rode down Brook Street with their mounted brass band, led by their drum major, to their camp on the Castle Green. Note the 'Tramways Express parcels' van on the left.

The mouth of the Tay, with its dangerous shifting sand banks was the scene of the grounding of many ships, including the SS *Fair City*, seen ashore at West Ferry beach on 19th October 1935.

SS *Dundee* ashore, at low tide, on Green Scalp off Tentsmuir Point 20 April 1935. In historical times, sixty ships of loot – the proceeds of the sacking of Dundee in 1651 by General George Monk – were all sunk within sight of the Broughty fishermen … is this treasure still lying offshore? Scottish Natural Heritage, in the summer of 2002 commissioned a survey of the seabed by the latest underwater equipment. Since then all has been quiet – although one report stated that positive readings for precious metals had been obtained. So far all that has been found is one cannonball.

The driver was the only person injured when this double-deck Alexander's bus (R71) skidded spectacularly into the wall of the Taypark Hotel on Dundee Road. In front of the bus, the lamp standard has, not a lamp, but a blue police light on top, which would flash to call the beat 'bobby' to his nearest phone.

In January 1937, this was the scene in Fairfield Road, West Ferry. Sand was blown off the beach and made passage difficult until cleared by the council.

Motor vehicles abandoned in a heavy snowstorm which left Fairfield Road, West Ferry, with drifts up to three feet deep. On this occasion muscle power was necessary to remove the unseasonable March 1937 snow!